Building a Lava Lamp

Published in the United States of America by Cherry Lake Publishing
Ann Arbor, Michigan
www.cherrylakepublishing.com

Reading Adviser: Marla Conn MS, Ed., Literacy specialist, Read-Ability, Inc.
Book Design: Jennifer Wahi
Illustrator: Jeff Bane

Library of Congress Cataloging-in-Publication Data

Names: Rowe, Brooke, author.
Title: Building a lava lamp / Brooke Rowe.
Description: Ann Arbor : Cherry Lake Publishing, [2016] | Series: My science
    fun | Audience: K to grade 3.
Identifiers: LCCN 2015049393| ISBN 9781634710268 (hardcover) | ISBN
    9781634712248 (pbk.) | ISBN 9781634711258 (pdf) | ISBN 9781634713238
    (ebook)
Subjects: LCSH: Handicraft--Juvenile literature. | Science--Study and
    teaching (Elementary)--Juvenile literature.
Classification: LCC TT157 .R685 2016 | DDC 745.592--dc23
LC record available at http://lccn.loc.gov/2015049393

Printed in the United States of America
Corporate Graphics Inc.

About the illustrator: Jeff Bane and his two business partners own a studio along the American
River in Folsom, California, home of the 1849 Gold Rush. When Jeff's not sketching or illustrating
for clients, he's either swimming or kayaking in the river to relax.

Science Notes

Building a Lava Lamp explores the relationship between oil and water. In this experiment, fizzing tablets release carbon dioxide into a bottle of cooking oil, water, and food coloring. Bubbles of colored water float to the surface, pop, and sink back down, replicating the appearance of a lava lamp.

Have you ever seen a **lava** lamp? It's bright. It's colorful. It's fun to stare at.

There are shapes inside it.
The shapes move.
The shapes change.

Do you think we can make a lava lamp?

Let's find out!

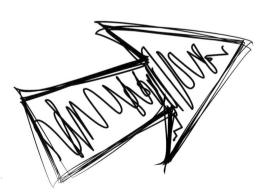

- Cooking oil
- Water bottle
- Water
- Food coloring
- **Fizzing tablets**

You will need these things

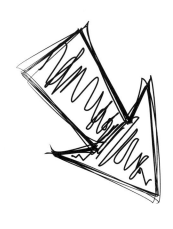

Pour the cooking oil into the water bottle. Fill the bottle halfway up.

Pour water into the bottle.
Leave space at the top.

Add some food coloring to the bottle.

Break one fizzing tablet in half. Drop one half into the bottle.

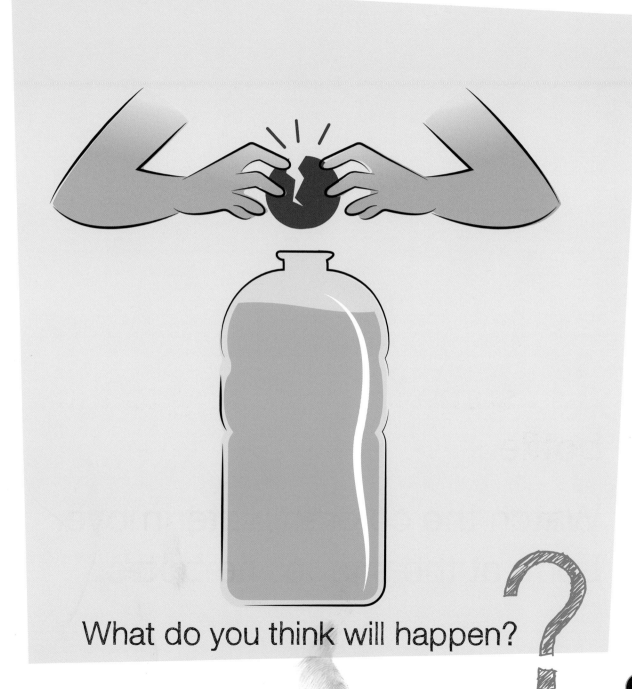

What do you think will happen?

Watch the colored water move.
Look at the shapes it makes.

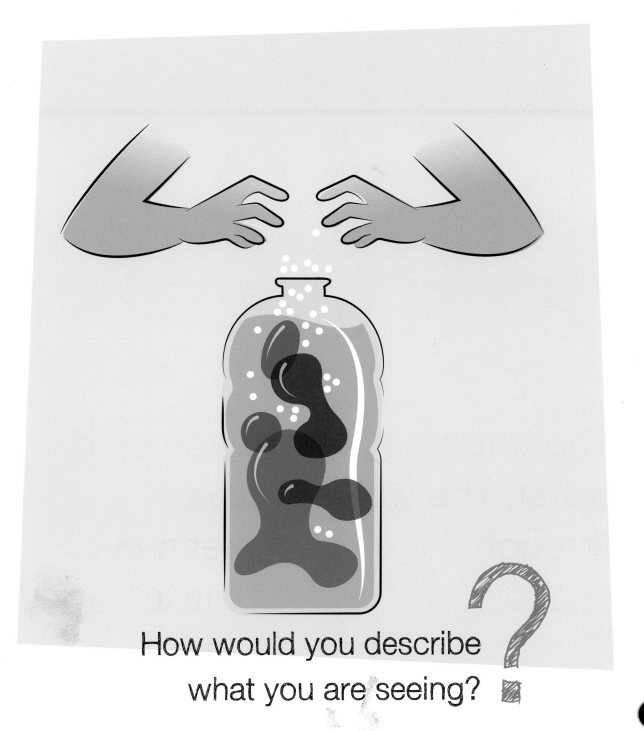

How would you describe
what you are seeing?

The **bubbles** push the colored water. The water moves through the oil. It makes fun shapes.

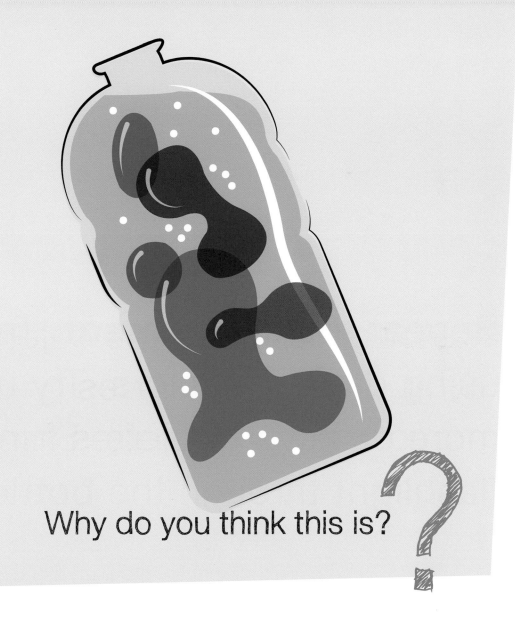

Why do you think this is?

Repeat the **experiment**. Try using different colors. Try using more or fewer tablets. Shine a flashlight through the bottle.

Try different colors!

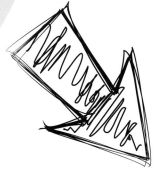

Good job. You're done!
Science is fun!

What new questions do you have?

glossary

bubbles (BUH-bulz) round balls of air inside a liquid

experiment (ik-SPER-uh-ment) a scientific test performed in order to learn something

fizzing tablets (FIHZ-ing TAB-lehts) small, solid pieces of medicine that dissolve in water

lava (LAH-vuh) the hot liquid rock that pours out of a volcano when it erupts

index